D1356018

Discovering What Goldfish Do

by Seymour Simon

WORLD'S WORK LTD

Kingswood and London

DISCOVERING WHAT GOLDFISH DO

Copyright © 1970 by Seymour Simon and Jean Zallinger
All rights reserved
First published in Great Britain 1973 by
World's Work Ltd
The Windmill Press, Kingswood, Tadworth, Surrey

Printed by offset in Great Britain by
William Clowes & Sons Limited
London, Beccles and Colchester

SBN 437 74651 8

Contents

1
Goldfish: Plain and Fancy

Each year, millions of goldfish are sold as pets. Not only can you buy goldfish in pet shops, but you will often find them for sale in department stores, circuses, and fairs. Goldfish are popular pets for good reasons. They are easy to keep, take up only a small space, and are interesting and fun to watch.

Pet shops usually have a number of different kinds of goldfish. Some goldfish are not even gold but white, blue, red, or black. Some are speckled with many colours. Some goldfish have large scales.

Others have small scales that are difficult to see. You'll find goldfish with long fins and short fins, with google eyes, with large heads, and with different shapes. Yet all of these different breeds are still goldfish, just as all the different kinds of dogs are still dogs. The scientific name of the goldfish is *Carassius auratus*. *Auratus* is from a Latin word meaning "golden."

The commonest type of goldfish has a long, arched body and a wide, short head. It has a forked tail fin, and its other fins are stiff and usually held away from its body. It may be gold, or white, or spotted with black. A slightly more ornamental breed is called the Comet. It has larger and more pointed fins than the common goldfish.

One-year-old common and Comet goldfish are about 1 to 2 inches long, not counting their tails. Goldfish don't grow very much when kept in a small tank. But in a large tank or in an outdoor pond, common goldfish grow to 7 or 8 inches in five years and over a foot in length when they are older. Goldfish can live for twenty years or longer.

Fantail goldfish have rounded bodies and divided tails that are not very long. Veiltail goldfish are like fantails but have divided tails and fins that are so long and full that they hang down in soft folds. Moors are shaped like veiltails but have pop-eyes and are all black in colour.

Other kinds of goldfish are Orandas, Lionheads, Shubunkins, Telescopes, and Celestials. These all have exotic heads or fins of different kinds.

Goldfish are related to the common carp. Wild goldfish are dull-silvery or brownish in colour. A few of them have golden sides. Wild goldfish are still used as food in China and other parts of the world. From fish such as these, the Chinese 1,000 years ago began to develop the domestic goldfish.

Goldfish were imported into England in the beginning of the eighteenth century. By the end of the eighteenth century, goldfish were common objects in fishbowls in many European countries. By the middle of the nineteenth century, they had reached the United States. In fact some goldfish had already escaped into a river in New York State by 1858. Nowadays, wild goldfish are found in parts of the United States, Europe, Asia, Australia, Hawaii, and large islands. Domestic goldfish are found all over the world.

2

Keeping Goldfish in Your Home

The common and the Comet goldfish are the easiest to keep at home. You can keep them in aquarium tanks or large fishbowls. They are hardy fish that can live all year long out-of-doors in ponds as long as the water does not freeze to the bottom.

About 1 inch of goldfish needs about 1 gallon of water in a proper aquarium tank. If you have a 5-gallon tank for example, you could keep one 2-inch and one 3-inch goldfish or five 1-inch goldfish or another combination totalling 5 inches. Don't count the tail when measuring the length of the fish.

This rule does not apply to fishbowls which have a narrow neck. Fill such a bowl to its widest point only. With this kind of bowl, every inch of gold-fish needs about 24 square inches of water surface area. To find the water surface area in a rectangular bowl, multiply the length of the bowl at the water level by the width.

To find the water surface area of a round bowl, measure across the bowl at the water level. Take half of this number and multiply it by itself. Multiply that result by 3 ⅐. For example, suppose your bowl is 8 inches across. Half of that is 4 inches.

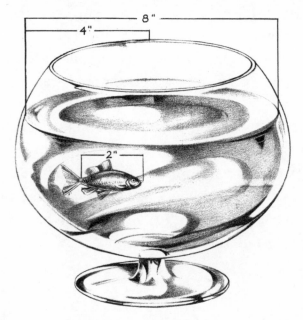

Multiplying 4 by itself you get 16. Multiplying 16 by 3 $\frac{1}{7}$ you get a little over 50 square inches. This would be enough for two inches of goldfish.

Overcrowded goldfish spend their time at the top of the water with their mouths partly in the air. The gulping sounds they make are their efforts to breathe. Smaller and fewer goldfish or a larger tank will answer this problem. The gulping may also be caused by polluted water. If this is the case, you will need to clean the tank.

Before you buy goldfish and bring them home, it's a good idea to prepare the tank for them. Wash the tank with water but not with soap. Even a small trace of soap will kill your fish. You can use salt to scrub at dirty spots. Rinse the tank well when you're finished.

You can keep your fish in a bare tank with water. But plants make a tank look nicer and are good for the fish too. Plants take in waste products, such as carbon dioxide, that the fish give off and use these wastes to grow. Plants also give off oxygen which the goldfish need. The fish also nibble at the leaves of plants getting some food in this way.

Some good plants to use in an aquarium are Cabomba, Elodea (also called Anacharis), Vallisneria, and Sagittaria. Healthy plants are green and crisp. You can buy plants at the same place you buy the goldfish.

Place a 1-inch layer of coarse, washed aquarium gravel at the bottom of the tank. This will anchor the roots of the plants. In most places you can use tap water in your aquarium. Ask the man at the pet shop if you're in doubt. Fill your aquarium three quarters full of water.

Let the water stand for a day or two until it clears and the bubbles are gone. Now you can buy your plants. Spread out each plant's roots if it has any, and cover them with gravel. Plants without roots such as Elodea can be thrust into the gravel and held down, or just allowed to float freely.

When you bring your fish home, float their container in the tank for fifteen or twenty minutes. This will adjust the water temperature in the container to about the same as the water temperature in the tank. Open the container and gradually mix the water in the tank with the water in the container.

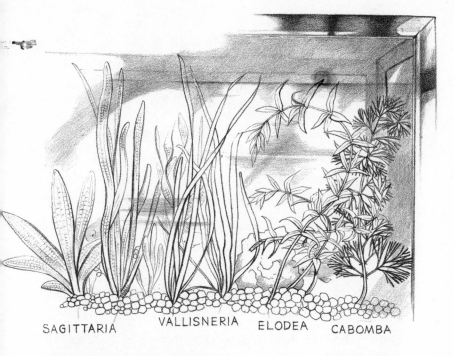

SAGITTARIA   VALLISNERIA   ELODEA   CABOMBA

Finally lower the mouth of the container and let the fish swim out into the tank.

You need not keep an aquarium near a window if you have a light in a reflector above the tank. If you do not have a light for your tank, keep the tank near a window where it will get some light. Don't put the tank where it will get direct sunlight for a long period of time. This will heat the water too much and will also make the water green. Goldfish

15

do well at room temperatures of about 50° to 80° Fahrenheit. Green water is caused by millions of microscopic plants called algae. Too much algae in the water and on the glass sides of the tank makes it hard to see your fish. Algae may also die and decay and turn the water into a smelly mess.

Feed your goldfish a small pinch of prepared fish food each day. Don't worry if you miss a day or two. Goldfish can go a long time without food. Feed only enough for the fish to eat it all in five minutes. Any excess food will decay and spoil the water. You can also feed your fish small bits of earthworms or small pieces of meat or fish. Remember not to over-feed. Remove any excess food before it decays.

Pet shops sell a long tube called a syphon. It's useful for cleaning bits of leftover food and dead plants from the top of the gravel. Add more water from time to time to make up for the water lost through evaporation. A well-planted tank that is not overcrowded with fish can stay for months without a complete water change.

3

The Outside and Inside of a Goldfish

Goldfish, like all fish, need to breathe air to live. Goldfish breathe by means of gills. Watch a goldfish swimming in a tank of water. It continually opens its mouth and takes in water. The water passes through gill chambers on either side of the goldfish's head and then out through the gill flaps.

Dissolved oxygen from air in the water passes through the thin skin in the gill chambers and into the fish's bloodstream. At the same time, a waste gas, carbon dioxide, passes out of the bloodstream

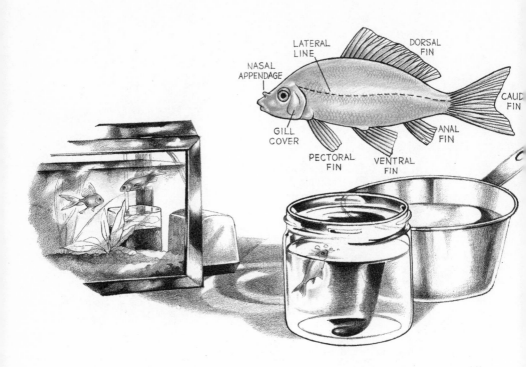

into the water. If there is not enough oxygen in the water, the goldfish comes to the surface and gulps air directly.

You can try this to see what happens to the goldfish when there isn't enough dissolved air in the water. Boil some water in a clean pan. This will drive out most of the dissolved air in the water. (Oxygen enters still water at the surface only very slowly.) Pour the water into a jar and let it cool undisturbed. When the water reaches room temperature, place a goldfish into it.

The fish begins to take in water quickly. Observe its rapid gill movements. In a short time the fish will suffocate unless it gets oxygen. If you have an aquarium air pump, use it to bubble air into the water. In a minute or two the fish will recover. Of course if you have no air pump, remove the fish promptly from the jar and replace it in its tank. It will get the needed oxygen from the tank water. Using an air pump in an aquarium allows you to keep twice as many fish in the same amount of space.

Goldfish can live for a considerable time out of water as long as their gills and skin remain moist. Thus if you have the use of a microscope or a magnifying glass, you can observe the circulation of blood in the goldfish's tail.

Here's what to do. Catch a goldfish and wrap its body and head in wet absorbent cotton wool so that only the tail shows. Place the fish on a glass plate with a little water to keep the cotton wool wet. Use a glass microscope slide to cover the fish's tail so that the tail is flattened and spread out. Examine the tail with a microscope or magnifying glass.

You'll see the blood moving through many blood vessels in the tail. In some of the blood vessels, called arteries, the blood will move quickly and in spurts. In others, called veins, the blood will move more slowly and steadily. The rapidly-moving blood comes from the heart. It contains digested food in a liquid form and the needed oxygen gas. The slower moving blood is returning to the heart. It contains carbon dioxide and other cell wastes.

The tiniest blood vessels you see, connecting arteries and veins, are called capillaries. After ten or fifteen minutes of observing, return the goldfish to the aquarium. If you handle it carefully, it should recover in a moment or two.

Goldfish have an air bladder or swim bladder within their bodies. They use the swim bladder to remain at any level in the water. A little more air in the bladder and a goldfish rises towards the surface. A little less air and it sinks towards the bottom.

Watch how a goldfish moves its fins to swim in the water. Sometimes it wig-wags its smaller fins like a paddle. This helps the fish to balance. At other times a goldfish bends its whole body and tail in short curves from one side to another. This makes them move quickly. How fast do goldfish swim? Scientists have timed goldfish moving about 3½ miles per hour.

The skin of a goldfish is covered with overlapping scales. Like the tiles on a roof, the scales cover the body, except for the head, in regular rows. One part of each scale is beneath the skin, while the other edge is free and can be lifted by hand.

Scales are hard and transparent. The colour of a fish is mainly due to cells underneath the scales. If you examine a scale from a fish (ask a fisherman for a scale—don't pull one from your goldfish!), you'll see a number of circular growth lines, depending upon the age of the fish. The scale grows at the edges. During warmer seasons when food is usually more plentiful, scale growth is more rapid. This results in wider growth lines. By counting the number of wider and narrower growth lines on a scale, you can tell the age of the fish.

Along each side of a goldfish is a line called a lateral line. The lateral line helps the goldfish sense the pressure of water around its body. Small currents or other water movements, moving objects in the water, or even fixed objects such as a rock or the glass sides of an aquarium that reflects pressure waves are sensed by means of the lateral line. In a darkened tank, a goldfish can swim about without hitting anything because of this sensitive line.

4

How Goldfish Reproduce

Goldfish can breed when they are about one year old. They can continue breeding till they are about six or seven years old. Out of doors, goldfish begin to lay eggs in the spring when the water temperature reaches about 60° Fahrenheit. At this time the body of the female goldfish swells up with the eggs carried in her body. The male looks slim by comparison.

Several days before the eggs are laid, the male goldfish begins to swim after the female fish. He drives her back and forth across the aquarium or

the pond. Finally the female sinks to the bottom.
In a short time she begins to release batches of her
eggs in the water. The eggs are released ten to
twenty at a time and may total up to 1,000 or more
at a spawning, or egg-laying.

As the eggs fall in the water, the male goldfish
spreads sperm cells over them. The sperm cells
unite with the egg cells, fertilizing them. Each egg
is about $\frac{1}{16}$ of an inch across, and is a pale
brown. The eggs are covered with a sticky sub-
stance that attaches to plant leaves.

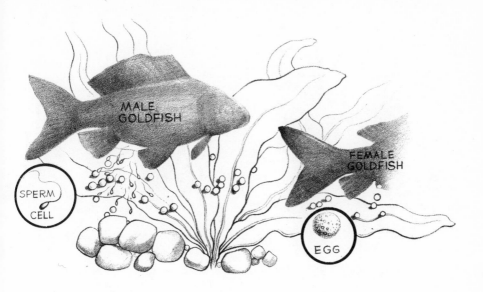

Spawning lasts a few hours, usually starting in the morning and ending in the early afternoon. Goldfish eat any of their eggs that they find. So if you are interested in having the eggs hatch and raising the fry, either remove the goldfish or remove the plants containing the eggs to another aquarium.

The eggs hatch in 4 days to about two weeks depending upon the temperature of the water. You can experiment to see how temperature affects the hatching time. Place several eggs and some water in each of three jars. Place one of the jars in your

refrigerator (not in the freezer part). Place another jar in a cool, shady spot outside your window. Keep the third jar at room temperatuare in the low 70s. Check the eggs in each jar every day. How long does each take to hatch? Do the eggs hatch when the temperature is very low? Do you think the temperature can be too high? How can you experiment to find out?

Other factors may also affect the time it takes for the eggs to hatch. Experiment to see if crowding of eggs in a jar has any influence on the time. Eggs need oxygen to develop. Crowding may lessen the

26

amount of oxygen available for each egg. You might also experiment with the effects of direct sunlight on hatching time. Can you think of any other conditions that might be important?

One scientist found that if eggs are kept out of water in a moist cloth for a day or two after spawning, then are placed in water again, they hatch sooner than eggs left in water the whole time.

When the egg hatches, the young fish called "fry" are about ⅕ of an inch long. They look like a thin thread attached to a fat belly. The fat belly is a

FRY
DETAIL

yolk-sac. It contains food which the fry uses for the first two days after hatching. At this stage the fry rest on the bottom or on the leaves of plants. They get all the food they need from the yolk.

But after about two days, the fry begin to swim about freely, searching for food. Their food consists of the microscopic animals found in pond water. In an aquarium, it's a good idea to add food to the water. One food you can use is the yolk of a hard boiled egg. Take a bit of the yolk and strain it through a fine nylon stocking. Feed the fish a drop or two, three or four times a day. You can also use strained boiled oatmeal for food. As the fish grow, switch to larger sizes of food.

At this time you can experiment to see if one type of food such as egg yolk produces quicker growth than another type of food. You can also check to see if crowding has any effect on growth. Other experiments might study the effects of light, temperature, and size of tank on the growth of the fish.

5

The Senses of Goldfish

You have organs such as your eyes and ears which sense your surroundings. Sense organs contain special kinds of cells called nerve cells. Each kind of nerve cell is sensitive to a particular message. Nerve cells in your eyes are sensitive to light, nerve cells in your ears are sensitive to sound, other nerve cells are sensitive to touch, and so on.

Goldfish too have senses. They can see, hear, smell, and feel many different kinds of things. For example, goldfish will dart away if you move your hand towards them suddenly. They will respond if you tap on the glass of the aquarium. They will respond in different ways to many of the things around them.

Here's how you can test to see if goldfish hear things. You will need a bell or some other kind of noise maker. Feed your goldfish each day at one corner of the aquarium. Ring the bell or make another noise as you put in the food. Do not put in any food unless you ring the bell. After a number of days, try just ringing the bell. The fish will rise to be fed even without your putting in the food. Can you see how this shows that goldfish respond to sounds?

You can try the same experiment but substitute a torch for the bell. After a while, the goldfish will rise to be fed whenever you flash the light. At this point, you might be interested in finding out more about a goldfish's sense of sight. For example, can a goldfish distinguish between colours?

Test this by placing a sheet of blue cellophane over one torch and a sheet of red cellophane over a similar torch. Try to make sure that the

same amount of light (but of course a different colour comes from each.

Place the red light on one side of the aquarium and the blue light on the other side. Put both lights on but feed only at the red light side of the aquarium. Switch the positions of the red and blue lights every few days. This is to be sure that the fish are responding to the colour of the light and not just to the location. After many trials the goldfish should go to the red light side of the aquarium when the lights are switched on.

Experimenters have found that goldfish can tell the difference between red and blue and between many other colours. They can also tell the difference between shades of grey. In fact, a goldfish's colour vision is much like that of man. A goldfish relies on its sight for getting food, for avoiding enemies and danger, for finding its mate, and for many other kinds of behaviour.

Goldfish also seem to be keen judges of water temperatures. In one experiment, scientists set up a tank with a switch that a goldfish could touch. When the switch was touched it lowered the temperature of the water slightly. The goldfish kept the water temperature in the tank within a few degrees of 75° Fahrenheit.

Here's how you can see how water temperatures affect goldfish. You will need a thermometer, a wide-mouthed jar with a top, some ice, and some hot water. Put the ice in the jar and cover it. Float the jar in the goldfish's aquarium until the temperature goes down to 65° Fahrenheit. Remove the jar and keep count of the number of times a goldfish swims back and forth across the aquarium in one minute. Do this several times and get the average for one minute.

Now place some hot water in the wide-mouthed jar, cover it, and place it in the aquarium. Remove the jar when the temperature in the aquarium reaches 80° F. Count the number of times a goldfish swims back and forth in one minute at this temperature. Is there a difference in swimming speed at the different temperatures?

A goldfish is a cold-blooded animal. That means its body temperature is not constant. It varies with the temperature of the surrounding water. Can you see why you might expect a goldfish to behave differently when the temperature around it changes?

Goldfish respond to other things around them. For example, one scientist reports that goldfish seem to swim more actively in a smaller tank than they do in a larger one.

You may notice other things about the way your goldfish behave. Record your observations and try to think of ways of finding out more about their behaviour.

6

Goldfish in Groups

Goldfish do not swim in schools the way many other fish do. Yet goldfish do behave differently when kept by themselves from the way they do when kept with several other companions. For example, a single goldfish in an aquarium usually swims faster than it does when kept with one or more companions.

You can estimate the speed of a single swimming goldfish by counting the number of times it swims back and forth in one minute and then multiplying by the length of the aquarium tank. For example, if the aquarium is 2 feet long and the goldfish swims back and forth ten times in one minute, then the fish is swimming at 20 feet per minute. Do this several times and take the average speed per minute. Place several other goldfish in the same aquarium as your first subject and then estimate its speed again. Perhaps being with other goldfish has a certain calming effect on an individual.

Goldfish also seem to grow more rapidly when kept with others of their kind than when they are kept by themselves. In fact, goldfish will grow more rapidly if kept in water in which other goldfish have lived than they do if put into clean water each day.

The reason for the better growth in groups is

DAPHNIA
ENLARGED

not certain but here are two theories that scientists have. When a few fish in a group find a large amount of food in nature, they seem to automatically spit up some of it. These food bits are taken in by some of the others. This results in a kind of food sharing among the group.

Another reason has to do with the mucus-covering a goldfish has over its body. This may contain certain substances which dissolve into the water and make it a better place for the goldfish to live in and grow.

When a large amount of food is always present in an aquarium, goldfish kept in groups even eat more than goldfish kept singly. You might be able to experiment with this in this way. You will need a medicine dropper and a large amount of Daphnia, a tiny water animal often sold as goldfish food.

Keep a group of three or four goldfish in one tank and a single goldfish in another tank. With the medicine dropper, feed the Daphnia to the single fish one at a time until it appears to lose interest in eating. You can count the Daphnia as you drop them in the tank, one by one. Now try the same procedure with the group of fish. Divide the number of Daphnia you feed to the group by the number of fish kept together. This will allow you to compare the average number of Daphnia eaten by each fish in the group, to the number of Daphnia eaten by the single fish.

Keep records for several days. You might then try exchanging one fish in the group for the single fish. This is to make sure that your results are not just due to a single fish that is not a good eater. It might be fun to report your results to your classmates, a science club, or by letter to an aquarium magazine.

Groups of goldfish behave differently in many other ways as well. For example, goldfish seem to learn faster in groups than they do individually. In addition, a goldfish that has learned something, such as a path to a feeding place, is rapidly imitated by other fish around it. You might say that goldfish can play "follow the leader." You can look into this further by performing some of the experiments in the next chapter using single fish and then using small groups of fish.

7

When Goldfish Learn

In a large fishpond, goldfish soon learn to come to the spot where they are fed. If they are fed at the same time each day, the goldfish gather from all over the pond just before the feeding period.

In aquariums too, goldfish soon learn their way about. They quickly learn that food is thrown in from the top of the tank, and they rise to that spot if you hold your hand over the water and wriggle your fingers.

Goldfish can be trained to respond to a sound or a light at feeding time (see p. 30). They can even be trained to respond in odd ways to some kind of signal.

For example, suppose you want to train a goldfish to swim through a hoop when you blow a whistle. Here's how to go about doing it. But remember, it takes much longer for a goldfish to learn a trick than a dog or a cat. So you have to be patient and keep at it.

You will need a large plastic loop such as the one in a soap bubble set, a whistle, and some pellets of food that your goldfish seems to like. Begin by blowing the whistle and dropping a pellet of food into the water. Do this several times a day. After a number of days, the fish will come to the surface for the food when it hears the whistle.

Now tie the plastic loop in place below the water. You may need an extension on the handle. Watch the fish swimming around the tank. Wait until you see it swim near the hoop. Immediately blow the whistle and drop a bit of food into the water. Keep repeating this. Blow the whistle and drop in food only when the fish is swimming near the hoop. Remove the hoop at the end of the feeding period.

Soon the fish will spend most of its time swimming around the hoop whenever it is placed in the water.

Now wait until the fish swims through the hoop before you blow the whistle and drop in food. After a few weeks of this kind of training, you should be able to blow the whistle and have the fish swim through the hoop. Remember to reward the fish each time it performs the trick. Otherwise it will soon stop performing for you.

Of course the fish does not really know what is happening. It is just swimming through the hoop at the whistle because that seems to produce food. This kind of training is often used with other animals such as dogs or horses.

After you've trained one goldfish, you may be interested in placing another in the same tank with the trained fish. You may find that the second fish begins to learn to swim through the hoop fairly rapidly. In a certain way, the second fish seems to be imitating the actions of the trained fish.

How does learning help a goldfish? In nature, goldfish are better off if they change their behaviour in response to changes in their surroundings. This change in their behaviour is what we call learning. A fish that learns is often better able to get food and avoid its enemies.

8
Goldfish Out-of-doors

Goldfish look so pretty in an aquarium that you might think they are just the fish to let loose in a nearby river or lake. Don't do it! Letting loose a pet to live in nature is almost always a mistake. They often make life difficult for native animals and may even cause their disappearance from the locality.

Goldfish are bottom-feeders. They stir up the water and the mud as they nose around for their food. Lots of feeding goldfish turn the water thick with stirred-up soil particles. This often stops the breeding of native fish and sometimes results in their death. Goldfish will also eat any fish eggs that they come across.

In addition, goldfish in nature don't even stay beautiful. Ornamental goldfish with large fins and bright colours are the least likely to survive in nature. Their large fins make them slow-moving, and their bright colours make them easy to spot. That's not a very good combination for long life in the wild.

In a few years all the pretty-looking goldfish disappear and only drab-looking goldfish with their terrible eating habits are left. You can see why goldfish can easily become pests when they are allowed to escape from aquariums and goldfish ponds.

On the other hand, goldfish are fine for small goldfish ponds, where they cannot escape. Here they can live all year round as long as the water does not freeze solid. Goldfish can survive if just the top of the pond freezes. They will breed each spring and, if there are plants in the pond for hiding, the young goldfish will grow into adulthood.

Goldfish have enemies out-of-doors. There are many animals that make fine meals out of any goldfish that they can catch. The list of goldfish enemies includes grass snakes, herons, kingfishers, otters, owls, and large frogs. Around cities or other built-up places, cats and rats are particular enemies of goldfish.

Despite all these and other hazards, goldfish are usually raised in outdoor tanks by wholesale fish breeders. They sell them by the millions each year. Many are sold for only 15p or 20p each. Yet some of the very exotic kinds of goldfish go for prices up to fifty pounds.

COMMON GOLDFISH

VEILTAIL

COMET

CELESTIAL

BRAMBLEHEAD or LIONHEAD

Goldfish are wonderful animals for many behaviour studies. They are inexpensive, take up only a small space, and readily show responses to sounds and sights. Many goldfish have weird and beautiful shapes and are interesting just on account of that. Goldfish are fine pets to keep, study, and enjoy.

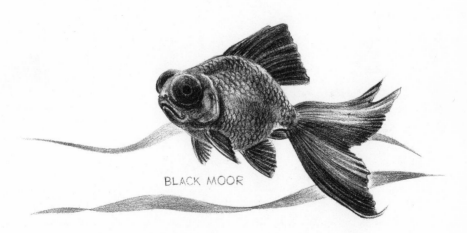

BLACK MOOR